Crash Course Freelance Writing

Robin Bull

DEDICATION

There just isn't enough room to thank my husband, Danny, for all of his support.

CONTENTS

Introduction

Hi. My name is Robin Bull and I am a full time freelance writer. When I say I am a freelance writer, I don't mean that I am between jobs and I'm using a skill and talent to try and pay my bills. I mean that writing is my profession and I work anywhere that there is an Internet connection. I mean this is my bread and butter. You're wondering, "Who the hell is she? I've never heard of her!" Well, of course not. I spend most of my writing time developing web content, professional industry articles, professional industry blogs, and ghostwriting. It's okay that you don't know who I am. When someone at a get together asks what I do and I respond with, "I'm a professional writer," I am suddenly the most interesting person in the room.

I am married and the mother of three great boys. My husband is, quite possibly, the most understanding man on the planet. I am very blessed to have someone that understands that just because it is "only" writing doesn't mean it is always an easy job. It takes some serious brain power.

In my former professions, I've worked as an administrative assistant, office manager, insurance defense paralegal, property law paralegal, bankruptcy analyst, and adjunct college instructor. I've also held down jobs in call centers. My point being that it really does not take an expensive graduate degree in order to become a professional writer. I am not knocking a good education. However, if Bill Gates and Steve Jobs could start the most famous of technology companies without college, you can become a writer. There is just something to be said for talent. For the record, I do have a BS in Paralegal Studies. Education, even if it means you just make it a life mission to learn something every day, is a powerful weapon.

This book isn't aimed at being some sort of freelance writing Bible. There's actually one out there. It's really good and comprehensive. I suggest you pick it up. This book is a crash course with information on what to charge, what to do, and where to find your opportunities. Hence the name of the book... The low fee attached to the book is really only to cover the time it took me to pull it all together. Past that, it's a labor of love.

Making the Leap

Some freelance writers get their start in the industry because they lost their job. Then, they get a contract, but it's not steady work. Most people don't have the money to invest in the proper books that have lists of possible work contacts. Most of them get overwhelmed by scams when searching for writing opportunities online.

So if you are working and reading this, start investing in books now. On my shelf I have Writer's Market 2010, Writer's Digest University, Novel & Short Story Market 2010, Poet's Market 2010, and Writer's Market 2013. I did not buy them at list price or all at once. I bought them all at Half Price Books. The most I spent was $10 on any one book on my shelf.

If I had to pick one must have from the list, it would be Writer's Market 2010. In it you will receive a code for a one year subscription to the Writer's Market website which is a $40 yearly value. So then in addition to the book, you will receive access to more updated listings of magazines, agents, and publishing houses.

Don't get discouraged if you don't have the money or a job to buy these books. I will give you an entire list of places to find potential opportunities on the web (all of the places are free).

The best thing to do is to start building your client list before you leave for the full time freelance path. You can start freelancing part time…if you're serious about it. We make time for what we really want. There's time that can be taken away from Facebook, Twitter, or sitting mindlessly in front of the TV. If you want to be successful, you have to put in the work to be successful.

Figure out your personal definition of success. My definition isn't the same as your definition. My definition isn't totally based on dollar signs. I can work wherever I want that has an Internet connection. Really, I don't need an Internet connection for most of my projects. If I've printed off my subjects then I can sit in the park with a notebook. I don't need the Internet until I send my projects back to their respective owners. I don't have to go and sit in a cubicle all day. If I want to take a break, I technically can…but that's time I am not getting paid. There are always two sides to every situation and decision. I can take a nap during the day and work at night. I can go to any school function or take my mother to the doctor. We all have the same 24 hours during the day. The difference is that as a freelance writer, I have more freedom to move around my responsibilities.

Professional writing is not for everyone. While writers are as varied as the topics to be written about, it doesn't mean that every writer can do this on a full time basis. Talent and writing skill only take a writer so far. You must have dedication, time management, and perseverance. It is a business, after all. Talent and skill alone won't pay the bills. You won't have someone over your shoulder making sure that you complete your assignments. That's your job. Freelance writing requires business sense to be able to turn it into a full time venture that pays the bills.

Granted, money isn't the only measuring stick of success. I measure personal success on how happy I am to be writing full time. Some writers measure success on their number of published pieces or how many pieces they've sold. All of those things are perfectly acceptable.

Schedule, Schedule, Schedule

Some of you reading this are anxious for me to jump straight to giving you a great starting list of potential opportunities. Clearly, writing work is important if you plan to make your living as a writer. More important than that is the fact that you need a schedule. Stop whining. I promise you'll be fine…unless you skip this section. If you skip this section and you aren't naturally driven to meet deadlines, I know you'll read this section after you've lost your first client due to your inability to stick to a schedule.

I know some of the whines include how you didn't want or don't need a schedule. First, professional writing isn't for those who can't stick to a schedule. It's fine to be free spirited and write where ever you want. Yes, situations come up that require us to be flexible with our time. I've written from emergency rooms, bars, McDonalds, and school parking lots just to name a few odd writing locales.

I promise you: if you don't set up a schedule you will fail because you will think you always have time to do a project (until it's too late) or you will allow your friends and family to guilt you into doing all of their personal errands. Because, hey, you can write whenever you want…including when you should be sleeping because you did their errands all day. That creates a snowball effect. You fall behind on all of your writing jobs because you spent your time taking care of the responsibilities that belong to others. It can, will, and does happen.

What many people (including new writers and their families) fail to realize about this industry is that it is primarily deadline driven. Companies that require web content, ad copy, articles, blog posts, PRs, or any other form of words in a document have a deadline for those words. Granted, it may not be a hard deadline. I have a client that will send me topics on a Monday and say, "Oh, you know, just sometime next week is fine." However, I still have the responsibility of managing my time to turn out the content. People won't pay you for not meeting a deadline. They have goals to meet. Agents, publishing houses, and other forms of publication also have deadlines for submissions or queries. If you don't meet those deadlines, you don't get published (or you don't get the opportunity to be published). You can't meet those deadlines without some form of writing schedule.

If you have a deadline for an article, you need time to research, write, and edit it. Use your time wisely. I can usually research, write, and edit a 700 word article in about an hour. That wasn't always the case. It still isn't always the case. It depends on my comfort level with the subject matter.

When I have a deadline of one week, I do what I can to write out my schedule in a manner that will allow me to make the deadline. No, it doesn't take me an entire week to write an article. However, I do have other clients. I don't necessarily schedule out specific time for each client, but I do schedule blocks of time to write.

My schedule is generally[1] as follows:

Monday – Friday

- 7:00 am – Wakey, wakey…eggs and bakey….well, minus the breakfast. I don't generally eat breakfast.
- 7:30 am – I leave to check in with a local client. I assist with research and drafting. During the time I'm with the local client, I also check my email, jot down notes, and I work on projects for other clients if I'm not needed.
- 12:00 pm – Come back to the house and start writing.
- 2:00 pm – I take a break.
- 4:00 pm – If I have more projects, I work on them. Otherwise I spend some time working on pet projects or researching gigs.

---

[1] Generally meaning that I've gotten to a point that if I don't have a hard deadline and I don't want to get up, then I'm going back to sleep. One day you will have that luxury, too.

I work on Saturdays as well. You should probably know that there are some days I work until 10:00 pm or even later.

Some of you are scratching your heads and rethinking your dream about becoming a freelance writer. You probably don't like that being your own boss will require a schedule. I promise that there is a method to the madness. Here's what you don't know just from looking at the schedule listed above:

1. Creating a block of time specifically for writing (and sticking to it) stops others from stealing your time. When you are running errands for others, you are inhibiting your cash flow and your client list ceases to grow because you are not available to answer inquiries or apply for writing jobs. So, this schedule protects your potential income flow and helps you grow your business.

2. Creating a block of time specifically for your writing will make you feel more professional. Your hours don't have to match my hours. I like to stay busy. I thrive on it. I've learned to see my extreme ADD (I was diagnosed in the early 1980s before it became a common diagnosis) as something that is to be utilized and treasured. You can work any hours that you want, but you should find a schedule to try and stick to for your own benefit. It can be detailed down to the minute or it can be relatively loose. My detail is actually far more scheduled then what is listed above. Remember, you will have clients that need your attention outside of that schedule.

3. Some days I ignore my schedule unless there is an absolute deadline. Usually I am able to turn around projects before they are due to the client. That's why I'm able to do this. If my mother needs to go to the doctor or I want to sleep in or go to a movie, I can do that. It is imperative that new freelancers don't make a habit of this. It's far too easy to get into the habit of procrastination or being a habitually late with projects when you're new.

4. Those hours don't necessarily mean I am stuck at home or in any one place. I love to work from the different libraries in my city. I am also known to work at fast food locations, parks, and sometimes even just sitting in my truck near a lake.

5. Those hours aren't always filled with work. Once you are used to the needs of certain clients, you turn those projects around much faster. In the beginning of my freelance career, it would take me almost an hour to research and draft a 700 word article or landing page. I would scrutinize and re-write it over and over again (thus taking away a job from some poor editor). Now? It takes me about 30 minutes or so for most 700 word projects even if I need to optimize it for the search engines.

Pricing

One of the things I hear most often from new or aspiring freelance writers is that they don't know what to charge. The answer isn't always so cut and dry.

First, let me start with a warning. Do not take slave wages. By slave wages I mean ridiculous offers you will see in some of the postings that are part of the job area of this course. There are some people who just do not want to budget for a writer. Don't let their ridiculous mentality rub off on you. When I say slave wages I mean $1 for 1,000 words. I mean $20 for a full length novel. Don't do that. The time you spend working on that project is time that you will lose money…and most likely your love of the craft. Again, don't do that. We are freelancers, but that doesn't mean that we can literally work for nothing. We still have bills. We still have a life (sort of). You can send a polite declination of their terms.

Now, with that out of the way you have about three options that you can use to determine your rate. You can even mix and match. I do want to issue another little piece of advice. Don't be afraid to negotiate a little in the beginning of your freelance career. I've bid $25 an hour on jobs and agreed to take $20 an hour. I've agreed to take as little as $10 an hour, but that was because I really believed in the project. I've taken tiny amounts on small copy jobs just to get the experience. The key word of that sentence was small. One more piece of rate advice…don't be afraid to bid on a project at your full rate. The worse they can do is hedge or say no. If they say no because of the price and you really want to participate in the project, negotiate. If not, ask them to keep you in mind for the future.

With that said, let's discuss the first method for rate setting. You start with a good old fashioned search on the Internet. Your goal is to find out what other freelance writers with your skill, talent, and experience charge for projects. Then, you adjust accordingly for your region. Remember that different projects may require different rates. You will also see per project, per word, and per hour freelance rates. It's a good idea to come up with a rate sheet that covers all three unless you plan to always refuse to accept projects on a certain basis. I use all three rates.

The next method involves a little more than just a guestimate of your worth. Get a copy of a good writer's manual. I used Writer's Market when I first started (great book – every writer should own one). Inside of it you will find charts that break down each common project, the rates (listed as low, average, and high), and whether it is done hourly or per project. It even gives you an idea about what people charge per word. A little hint about per hour: if you are a fast typist, don't screw yourself. I can do about 700 words in 30 minutes. So, if I have a landing page that I need to write and it's only 800 words and I charge around $11.00 an hour, I'm only going to get paid $5.50 for that work. If I have a lot of work from that client, it might be okay. The math involved in this paragraph leads me to the third method that is infected with math. Yeah, I didn't like the thought of math either, but it's a pretty simple method.

Simple math can help you determine what you should charge if you plan to only charge by the hour. First, decide how much you want to make in a year as a freelance writer. I am going to break this down to very, very basic levels. Why? Because I am math impaired and seeing it broken down to this level was very helpful for me. I am sure that all of you reading this don't have the math problems I do, but just in case…I'm going to walk you through this.

Let's say that you decide on the goal of $35,000.00 for a yearly income goal. For some, that may seem like a really low income. Here's a secret you may not know: when you work primarily from home, you save on a lot of expenses. Getting $35,000.00 a year is like $45,000.00 a year because you don't have many of the same expenses as those who hold traditional jobs.

Next, we divide by 12 because we have 12 months in a year. That's roughly $2,916.66 per month. Every month has four weeks. So, we take my monthly amount and divide it by four and now I have $729.16 per week.

Well, now we have to decide how many hours per week we want to spend writing. Those will be my billable hours. We will say that I plan to have 35 billable hours every week. You can say 40 hours or even ten hours if you want, but ten hours in the beginning of your career would be unrealistic. The weekly rate of around $729 divided by 35 billable hours is around $20.84 per hour. I generally round up. As of the publication date of this book, I average around $20.00 per hour. I live in an area that has a very low cost of living; for me, this is a reasonable rate.

Here are a few considerations when it comes to setting your price:

- Remember that you will have to pay taxes. You should take out around 25% or so of your earnings every week and set them aside in an account. Hire a good accountant to help you with your taxes.
- Don't charge $20 + an hour unless you are worth it. Be honest with yourself. Ask for feedback from your clients and adjust your rates and business accordingly.
- Consider setting per project rates.
- Don't forget to consider your own expenses when setting your rate.
- Charge fair rates. Don't take advantage of your clients. You want return work.

Getting Started

Another common question I get asked is how to get started as a freelance writer. It's easier than you think to get started, but it's not necessarily an easy field to work in. I don't say that to scare you away before you even get started. Honestly, there are plenty of jobs to go around because we are a consumer driven society…that and practically everyone except The Unibomber loves the Internet. That means that there will always be a market for freelance writers. There will always products to sell and web content to write.

First you need your business set up.

- You need a computer. It doesn't matter if it is a laptop or a desk top.

- You need Word or WordPerfect. I like Open Office, but it's not as compatible as people like to think. It doesn't always convert the document the way it should. If someone makes edits to your odt file in Word and sends it back to you, you may have a hard time accepting those changes without typing the entire document again. Microsoft offers a monthly payment plan to use Word if you can't afford to purchase it outright.

- You at least need Adobe Reader. There will come a time when you take a gig that involves turning a PDF file into a Word document. Hey – don't judge and never say never...because it will happen. Yes, there are other PDF readers out there, but Adobe Reader is free and can also sign documents. If you want Adobe Professional or if your client requires that you have it, Adobe also offers a monthly plan.

- You need a dedicated work space. I don't care if it's your kitchen table or a private office. Of course the great thing about owning a laptop is that you can work from pretty much any location. However, it can be very helpful to have a particular area that you will commonly use as your work space.

- You need at least one large flash drive. Back up all of your work onto the flash drive. Sadly, things happen to computers and even to CDs. A flash drive makes a great back up option. It also allows you to use it to work from another computer.

- You need a calendar. I have a desk calendar. It is divided into weeks. It's is about the size that teachers use to plan their weeks. I write down my gigs and the clients that provided the gigs. I also notate any deadlines or jot down notes. My calendar goes just about everywhere I do. I do have an iPod, but I don't use it for this purpose. It's much faster for me to just write it down.

- You need a writer's resume. Research different examples of a writer's resume on the Internet. You could hire someone to write your resume for you.

- You need a general writing cover letter. For each individual writing gig you submit your materials to, you should make sure that you customize the letter to match.

- You need a collection of your clips. Don't worry if you haven't been published. Use clips from your blog that are insightful and truly show your writing style. Start an account with Hubpages.com and write articles. You get one shot at a first impression.
- You need the schedule you set for yourself. Remember, it's okay to alter what you decided to use. It's okay to be flexible.

After you have those things put together, it's time to actually take a deep breath and start searching and bidding. I'll give you a great list of places to get started and tell you where to go to find your free bonus (free job listings to save you some work) soon. Until you have a set list of clients, you need to use your writing time to look for gigs and update your social media presence.

There will be places that turn you down…and that's okay. Guess what? Soon you will have so many writing gigs that you have to say no to people who come to you. That's a great problem to have, isn't it? It only took me about two months of constantly applying myself and turning in great writing to have that problem. Your choice at that point is turn it away, refer it, or subcontract it. Be careful if you choose to subcontract. That is a great way to get bit on the behind.

To continue this section, let's switch to actually getting started as a freelance writer. Many say they want to be a freelance writer. When they say that, they sort of mean it. They want to write for a living…but they dream of making a living by writing about the things of which they have a personal love. Honestly, I can't say that I know many aspiring fashion writers that would want to take an article about apicoectomies. Come to think of it, I can't think of many aspiring freelance writers that would even know what that is (unless they have a background in dentistry).

The cold, hard truth is that, at least initially, if you want to make a living as a writer then you have to take the writing jobs that pay decent money. Many people dream of writing novels or food blogs all day and receiving a big, fat check every month. Sadly, that's not reality. Novels need an audience that will buy the book. Then, you have to continue to churn out novels that people continue to buy. Sometimes (a lot of the time) you need an agent to get the attention of a publisher. Sure, you could self-publish, but that can bring about its own set of considerations.

Some of you are saying, "So? I expect problems and eat them for breakfast!" Well, that's great that you hold that kind of attitude. Just remember this: for every minute you spend writing and self-publishing, you lose money because you aren't out marketing what you've already published. For every minute you're marketing and not writing, you are potentially losing money because you aren't developing new work. Some publishing houses won't even talk to you unless you have an agent.

I've written articles for dentists, attorneys, dermatologists, and a dating website (among other professional and semi-professional gigs). I've ghostwritten novellas and short stories. I've written web copy. I've done copywriting (and I eventually learned to love it). I've done a lot of different writing gigs…and I didn't like all of them. In fact, I discovered that I hate writing novellas for other people because I tend to try and write what I think they want instead of doing what I was hired to do…writing the damn novella. However, I did learn something from every single writing gig.

Until you are busy enough that you can turn people away, the real factor on whether or not you should take a writing gig is whether you are capable of completing it. Whether or not you like it is a secondary consideration. Now, with that said I would like to clarify one thing: I am NOT advocating that you take jobs that would compromise your own morals or ethics. What I am saying is that if you are capable of good research, you can tackle a lot of writing gigs…more than you would possibly believe. I know more about sclerotherapy than even some people in the medical field. I've researched the procedure and ghostwritten articles about it more than 15 times.

Gigs that pay but that you aren't crazy about are commonly referred to as meat and potato jobs. I call them my rice jobs. I may not want it every day, but I have it because one day I'll need it. As you will come to find out, the industry is very much feast or famine. That is even truer if you paint yourself into the proverbial corner by not looking outside of your determined writing expertise. Like rice, these jobs fill a need…and they're not so bad even if I've been doing them for what seems a very long time. Like rice, there are many varieties…so you can get a little change when you need it. These are your staple jobs. You can continue to generate income and build your income up to the level you want while you look for writing jobs you love.

Some of you are saying, "I get that, but how do I break into the field I want?" First, you build credibility as a talented writer who is reliable. You can start a blog or website. I like buying websites that end with .info because they are inexpensive. Fortunately, the Internet is rapidly expanding and there are more extensions that are being released. You could start a blog for free. You could even get a page at hubpages.com and write on whatever topic you wish. Just make sure that the writing you provide on your site is top notch. That writing will become your portfolio until you have published clips. As you contact potential clients, use those particular articles as writing samples. I used hubpages.com for quite a while. I received many offers based off of sharing one of my better articles as my writing sample.

Alright, so now you have your schedule (or at least, you should have a general idea of when you will do your writing), you have a general idea of what you like to make (but please realize that when you look at jobs the amount you see will be lower), and you have your reality check. It's time to really get started and land that first gig.

Gig Finding Locales

Truthfully, you could ask 100 freelance writers about their favorite places to find gigs and you will get 100 different answers. This list is certainly not meant to be all-inclusive. As your career expands, websites will change. New websites will appear. You will have your own favorites.

First, you should realize that you are totally capable of finding freelance writing gigs without the Internet. Every business has a need for a freelance writer. Some may not know it or may have someone that is part of the business that handles the writing. Brochures, newsletters, policy and procedure manuals, standard letters, not-so-standard letters, ad copy, and website copy are just a few of the things that business owners need from writers. They may not need you now, but they may need you in the future.

Send a letter of introduction to small businesses in your area advertising your services and rates. Make sure to follow up. They don't know that you exist if you don't stay on their radar.

Of course with that said, you probably shouldn't just grab a hard copy of the yellow pages and start cold calling. I suppose you could do that, but imagine the time and the yelling and hanging up that would ensue. Are you sure your fragile writer's ego could handle that? Don't be offended. All writers are sensitive when it comes to their writing. You should target which businesses you want to contact. You should also let all of your friends and family know that you are accepting new writing clients.

Rejection is part of life. Rejection isn't a personal judgment on your work. Any job you applied for during your life that you weren't hired for was a form of rejection. It wasn't that your work was subpar. It's just that someone else was a better fit. There is plenty of writing work. Rejection isn't a measure of your writing ability. It's just that someone else's style is a better fit for that particular gig. That's good because it gives you time to pursue other writing avenues.

Twitter

Yes, believe it or not Twitter is a great place to find out about writing gigs. The key is to follow the right accounts. However, before you push the "Follow" button, check out their profile and make sure that they post legitimate jobs and that they aren't wanting you to sign up to learn their "system" to blog for money. Even if you were to sign up for someone's blogging business system, you still have to generate your own traffic.

Once you have found Twitter accounts that send out writing gigs, group them together as a list. That will make it easier for you to find the jobs that you may miss if you follow a lot of people on Twitter. Visit those profiles and Twitter will give you suggestions to follow. Check those profiles before deciding to follow them. Soon you will have a nice list of jobs that you can always rely on to find writing gigs. If you follow me on Twitter, you can see the list I have set up for writing gigs. My Twitter name is @TheRobinBull.

Tumblr

Tumblr, much like Twitter, can be used to find writing gigs. You can save certain tags (in addition to following certain accounts). Some of the best tags include calls for submission, writing opp, and even amwriting.

Facebook

It is important to use common sense when using Facebook to look for writing gigs. If it costs you money to get started, that's not a job. It's a business opportunity. You don't need to pay a fee in order to find writing jobs online. The only exception to this is if you were to pay for a membership to a legitimate site such as flexjobs.com. At that point, you're paying primarily for the convenience of not having to do your own extensive search for companies that would hire you on as an employee.

Facebook is brimming with groups for freelance writers, authors, and those wanting to work from home. It's also full of scammers. If an offer looks too good to be true or offers to "stuff your PayPal account with $20 deposits hundreds of times per day" then stay away from it. Jobs for ad posters are scams. They love to target new writers. I've had many people approach me online because of my profession and try to convince me that I could become rich by posting ads. Essentially, they post an ad promising to teach you how to get hundreds of dollars per day by posting ads. You click it, you send them $20, and then you post the exact same ad in the hopes some sucker will click it.

Find legitimate Facebook pages and groups to join for writers. Even writers groups and some fan pages do not offer legitimate opportunities. My favorite Facebook pages include:

- Facebook4Freelancers.com: Freelance Writing Jobs
- Freelance Writing Gigs

Yes, I have a page. I post jobs on my page from time to time.

- http://www.facebook.com/TheRobinBull

As you can see, I've really only offered you words of caution if you attempt to use Facebook to find writing gigs. The only way I've found legitimate opportunities on Facebook is from using the two pages listed above. That's not to say that all the other pages on Facebook are just scams. I'm just a firm believer on sticking with pages that I know are absolutely legitimate.

Indeed

Now that we've covered the basics of finding writing gigs on social media, let's look at other online avenues. I can't say enough good things about using indeed.com to look for writing gigs.

I love indeed.com because it is searchable. Above that, I can set up multiple searches and have the jobs emailed to me every single day. Here are a few of my searches that I have emailed to me every single day:

- Content writer
- Freelance writer
- Writer
- oDesk (more on that soon)
- eLance (more on that soon)
- Telecommute writer

Indeed.com does the job searching for you. It searches all of the major jobs sites and also sends jobs posted directly by the party looking for a writer. When you click on the links within the email, it will take you to the job posting on indeed.com. Some of the jobs allow you to apply directly from indeed. Others have the link back to the employer that needs the position filled. Additionally, you will find other jobs that are related to the job that you are reading. Indeed also offers the ability to store your resume online. It's free, easy, and yes there is an app for that.

Monster

This definitely works to find writing gigs, but I've had more luck finding permanent writing gigs with Monster than freelance gigs. Of course, your results will vary…because it is all about in the way you search (just like any job board).

The beauty of Monster is that you no longer have to set up an account in order to have jobs emailed to you. The down side is that it doesn't seem to be as focused as indeed.com. Currently I only use one search for Monster. I search for content writer jobs. Unfortunately, that brings back jobs that aren't related to content writing such as jobs in security.

TweetMyJobs

I am a new convert to the wonders of TweetMyJobs.com. You can set up job alerts to be emailed to you or even have the jobs tweeted directly to you. Another great feature is this little red button that appears when you visit a job link on their page. When you click the button, it tells you who you know (from your contacts on Facebook) that may know someone at that company.

I have one search set up for "writer." It brings back more than enough jobs for me to view. The site is incredibly easy to use.

ProBlogger

I am always amazed when I talk to aspiring freelance writers that ask if money can be made through blogging. The answer is yes…but what people don't tend to understand is that blogging for bucks is often done on someone else's blog. Many people seem to be taken aback by the fact that their name may not appear or that they won't receive guest blogger status. Well, we writers are often under recognized (unless they're dead…consider H.P. Lovecraft or all the poets who achieved literary success posthumously).

If you are a blogger looking to become a paid blogger, I highly recommend that you pay the $17 to join the community. He's not offering some "system" or business opportunity. It's kind of like paying for a service like flexjobs.com. You're paying for convenience. You could find out all of those things that you will need to know to reach your maximum potential as a paid blogger, but that could take a lot of time on your own since you would have to weed through the technological jungle. How much time do you have to devote to that? For $17 you have access to that information.

Now, the jobs board for Problogger is absolutely free to see and is located at http://jobs.problogger.com. He keeps the page updated and free of junk.

In fact, he takes down posts that he knows have been filled. The opportunities are broken down into categories such as Corporate, Miscellaneous, Co-Blogging, and more.

oDesk

In the world of freelance job sites that require bidding, oDesk is my absolute favorite. Why? First, it is totally free. You don't have to buy anything in order to bid and all proposals are created equal. You don't have to pay money or do anything special in order for your bid to be featured. Next, if you aren't chosen for a gig or if you withdraw your application from a gig you receive your application point back within 12 hours. You don't have to pay for tests. You simply complete tests to show your expertise.

Once you've passed the oDesk readiness quiz and confirmed your identity, you will be awarded with a certain amount of applications to apply for gigs. The most you can have is 25. Unlike other freelance sites, you don't wait until the end of the month for your applications to be replenished. They are replenished once certain criteria are met.

You can set up searches on oDesk and it will also set up a recommended job feed. You are not limited to just one area in which you can apply. If you have the expertise, you are eligible to apply. Time is tracked via a download called Time Tracker.

Most of my gigs come from oDesk. You'll be surprised at the types of gigs that you can find on oDesk. You can find everything from start-up companies to major marketing firms to agencies to law firms. The great thing is that jobs are added all the time.

The biggest pitfall on oDesk is that usually when people decide to use something like this they have this dream that they will make a ton of money. Well, you won't win every bid. You also will see a lot of companies and individuals offering what I call slave wages. If you read the following terms in the title of a gig, they will award it to the lowest bidder:

- Lowest bid wins

- New to oDesk welcome
- Entry level rates

Many of these people don't realize that the saying "If you think it's expensive to hire a professional, just wait until you hire an amateur" is true. They don't realize that writing is more than just plunking words into a document. Good writing, particularly writing that is meant to sell or gain rank on the search engines, must be carefully worded.

If you really want the experience with that particular client or that particular industry, you can most certainly bid low. My regular rate on oDesk is $18.00 / hour. More experienced freelance writers probably scoff at my rate. I chose that rate because I can easily live off of it in my area of the nation.

Another great feature of oDesk is that people with projects can invite you to apply or interview. It's great. If you have zero applications left and someone invites you to apply, you can still apply for their gig.

Another word of caution – oDesk offers flat rate projects. Flat rate projects are not guaranteed to be paid to you through oDesk. Please be very careful if you apply. You should always ask for a retainer or at the very least a milestone payment.

Take as many tests as possible to highlight your abilities. Fill out your profile and utilize the built in portfolio. Carefully word your profile to read like the professional writer that you truly are. Read and re-read it.

oDesk charges the client 10% or so of what you are paid as a fee. So, if the client posts a budget of $200.00, do your best to either bid at $200.00 or below (to include the fee). Be careful not to sell yourself short.

oDesk pays weekly. Weeks end on Sunday. Then, the clients have the opportunity to review the time log. Unless they alert oDesk to some sort of problem, your money will be available around Wednesday of the week following the review period. If you earned more than $100.00, oDesk will automatically transfer the funds provided that you set up your payment method. If you earned less than $100.00, you must go in manually and request your funds.

Freelancer

Freelancer.com is another bid for work site. It has its pros and its cons. I absolutely love the look of the site. I also love that I can set it up to email me multiple times per day when new gigs are added in certain categories.

Their website is also kind of like playing a video game. You level up by performing certain actions in order to gain more points to apply. You can use more of your points to bump your bid to the top. The difference between Freelancer and oDesk is that you have to use your points on Freelancer to take tests to show your capabilities…unless you want to give them real money (on top of the money they will take if you win a bid).

I think the look of the site is about the only jump it has over oDesk. While I do have an account on Freelancer, I don't bid on many jobs. Usually the invites I receive offer to pay me $1 for 1,000 words. At that point, I'm just losing money. Freelancer is excellent if you have an interest in academic research report editing or writing.

PeoplePerHour

Believe it or not, many people do not know about PeoplePerHour.com. It is a great site to find freelance work. Additionally, they pay very quickly.

Recently, I took a very small editing job (5,000 words). The person was a student (and no, it wasn't their research paper) and wanted some help from an "actual writer" to get the perspective of a reader and a professional. In short, I was paid to beta read a small project. I read it and did a small editing job. I included questions as the reader. Over all, the job took me less than two hours. I wanted to make sure that she understood the changes and the questions. The student had a budget of $50. I went in with an incredibly low rate of $18 simply because I knew how little of my time it would take…and I wanted to help. The student immediately put the money into escrow. When I returned the file, I went through the PPH system to invoice. They released my money to PayPal the very next day. PPH kept $3.00 of my $18.00. So, while their fee is a little high freelancers get the benefit of quick pay.

Another benefit of PPH is that you can set it up to connect with Facebook and embed it into your blog. If you have friends on PPH, you will know and you can endorse each other. They also offer emails for new gigs. They will send you an email with new gigs posted from every category that you are interested. It's very helpful. I don't have to spend all day going through gigs. They also have an app.

Like all the other freelance sites, PPH relies on the credit system. You get so many credits in order to bid on jobs. Once you use your credits you must wait until the beginning of the next period to bid.

eLance

eLance offers free and paid options. With the free option you get a certain number of "connects" (opportunities to bid) per month. They don't refresh if you withdraw or don't get the job. You can pay a monthly fee to receive more connects. You can use additional connects to be moved to the top of the bid list. If you refer new members, you can earn more connects. The best thing about eLance is its longevity. You know that they aren't going anywhere.

eLance gives you a profile and also allows you to see any area. As a free member, you can only bid in one category. Let's say you're a technical writer. So, of course you subscribe to the writing category. Let's say that one day you decide to look through the IT category just to see what's shaking in the world of freelance IT. Lo and behold you spot a job from a company that needs a technical writer. You can't bid on it as a free member because it's not in the writing category. As you can see, one wrong click from what could have been a potential client severely limits your ability as a freelancer.

eLance also pays weekly. They have the ability to wire the money straight to your bank account. eLance and oDesk are owned by the same company. The payment system offered through eLance can be a little frustrating...particularly if you take on gigs that are considered "crowd funded" or "crowd sourced."

eLance uses a time tracking download similar to what is used by oDesk.

Certain clients will not bill you from that (such as those involved in the crowd sourced work). That's okay. If it is a flat rate project, run the time tracker anyway. This will add the hours up on your profile. People are more apt to award jobs to freelancers that they can verify work hours. I do the same thing with my oDesk time tracker. I just mark it as "For my profile use – time tracking."

CareerBuilder

If you are looking for contract work or full time work (but still want the ability to work from home), you can try CareerBuilder.com. Clearly, it's not designed for strict freelancing use. However, many companies (particularly those in the communications industry) understand the value of a freelance writer. This is particularly true for those that wish to hire a freelancer on a long term contract.

You can set up a job alert to email you. I don't even have an official CareerBuilder.com profile. You don't need one to set up job alerts. My search terms for CareerBuilder:

- Freelance writer
- Content writer
- Telecommute writer
- Digital content

FreelanceWriting.com

There aren't enough good things in the world that I could possibly say about this particular site…and all of the other sites owned by the gentleman that runs FreelanceWriting.com. He also has a weekly newsletter that is free. It is delivered every Tuesday. It contains freelance jobs as well as information about what's new on his sites.

Jobs are updated weekly on FreelanceWriting.com. In addition, he has links to his many other sites that list calls for submission for contests, magazines, publications, and lots of other great stuff. His site was the first one I used to look for freelance work.

FreelanceWriting.com also offers great articles. Occasionally, he accepts and pays for articles related to the freelance writing lifestyle. If you visit his page, make sure and use the donate button. The FreelanceWriting.com family of websites is truly a blessing to all of us in the industry.

My second favorite site ran by the site owner is onlinewritingcareer.com.

FreelanceWritingGigs.com

FreelanceWritingGigs.com is another great freelance writing site. The owner of this site is a former English teacher. She updates her site daily and offers a free list of writing gigs. You can subscribe to her listings via email. She is incredibly friendly and has always been willing to answer any question I asked when I was new to freelance writing. Her Facebook fan page is phenomenal as well. You can find it listed underneath the Facebook section of this book.

SearchTempest.com

Many people feel skeptical when they look for writing gigs using Craigslist. Who could blame them? More than one person has been robbed because they answered a Craigslist ad. However, if you use some common sense you can find work on Craigslist.

SearchTempest.com takes the hard part of checking every city for writing gigs away from you. You type in your search term (I use the word "writer"), your zip code, and how far the cities can be (you can search all of them by checking the "any" box), and then click the button that will search all the gigs.

You will receive a customized search. As you read through the listings I ask that you report any ad that is a scam or inappropriate. Far too many scammers focus their attention on the writing community. Do your part by reporting their post.

I love using SearchTempest.com. It has made Craigslist a lot more manageable. It takes me about a week to go through every city. I leave it pulled up in a browser window of its own and just open the gigs I want to read in a new tab. Once I finish with a city, I click the tiny X near the right hand corner of that particular box of gigs.

Final Notes

Well, that's it in a nutshell. Now you know how to find a massive amount of freelance writing gigs. Remember, your schedule is your friend. You can write from anywhere you want. You can write whenever you want...with respect to the needs of your clients.

The websites listed here isn't meant to be an all-inclusive list of places to find gigs. In fact, if you have a smart device you should download iFreelancer and Freelance. Those can cut down your searching time. Granted, the application process isn't smooth. I usually just email any jobs I like to myself.

Make sure and visit the crashcoursefreelance.info every day. I post gigs on a regular basis as a thank you for purchasing this short book. Finally, remember that it takes time to get into the swing of things in any career and freelancing is not an exception to that rule. Get out of the house. Talk to other freelancers. Realize that this isn't just a career...freelancing is a lifestyle!

Questions? Comments? Concerns?

You may feel lost when you embark on your freelance writing career. The number of emails that show gigs may overwhelm you every day. You are not alone. If you have questions, comments, or concerns you can contact me in the following ways:

- Email   thepromiscuouswriter@gmail.com
- Facebook http://www.facebook.com/TheRobinBull
- Twitter   @TheRobinBull
- Voicemail 206-337-5925

- Website   http://www.crashcoursefreelancewriting.info (where you will find writing gigs posted on a daily basis – that's my thank you gift to you for buying this short guide)

ABOUT THE AUTHOR

Robin Bull is a full time freelance writer. She resides in Oklahoma City, Oklahoma with her husband, three sons, and dog. She likes to write in odd places and has an eclectic background.